PRINCEWILL LAGANG

Beyond the Search Box: Unraveling the Mind of Larry Page

First published by PRINCEWILL LAGANG 2023

Copyright © 2023 by Princewill Lagang

All rights reserved. No part of this publication may be reproduced, stored or transmitted in any form or by any means, electronic, mechanical, photocopying, recording, scanning, or otherwise without written permission from the publisher. It is illegal to copy this book, post it to a website, or distribute it by any other means without permission.

Princewill Lagang asserts the moral right to be identified as the author of this work.

First edition

This book was professionally typeset on Reedsy.
Find out more at reedsy.com

Contents

1. Beyond the Search Box: Unraveling the Mind of Larry Page — 1
2. The Architect of Tomorrow — 4
3. Legacy and Lessons — 7
4. Beyond the Search Box: Technology, Humanity, and the Future — 10
5. Future Horizons: Navigating the Unknown — 13
6. Reimagining Tomorrow: The Intersection of Technology,... — 16
7. The Uncharted Frontier: Exploring the Unknown — 19
8. The Tapestry of Tomorrow: Weaving a Shared Future — 22
9. Resilience in the Face of Disruption — 25
10. The Human-Tech Symphony: Crafting a Harmonious Future — 28
11. The Compass of Digital Ethics: Navigating the Moral... — 31
12. The Technological Renaissance: Crafting a Humanistic Future — 34
13. Summary — 37

1

Beyond the Search Box: Unraveling the Mind of Larry Page

The air in the room was charged with anticipation as Larry Page stepped onto the stage, his piercing gaze sweeping across the sea of faces. The auditorium lights dimmed, and the title of the presentation, "Beyond the Search Box," illuminated the giant screen behind him. The audience, a mix of tech enthusiasts, entrepreneurs, and curious minds, leaned forward in their seats, eager to unravel the mysteries of the man behind the world's most popular search engine.

The Genesis of a Visionary

The chapter opens with a glimpse into Larry Page's early life, tracing the roots of his brilliance. Born in East Lansing, Michigan, Page displayed an insatiable curiosity from a young age. We delve into his formative years, exploring the influence of his parents, both computer science professors, and the fertile ground of academia that nurtured his burgeoning intellect.

The narrative captures pivotal moments in Page's youth, from building his first computer out of spare parts to the time he hacked into the university's computer network, foreshadowing the unconventional path he would take in the world of technology.

The Stanford Connection

As Larry Page entered Stanford University, the chapter explores his encounter with Sergey Brin, a fellow computer science student who shared Page's fervor for pushing the boundaries of technology. The duo's collaboration on the Backrub project, a precursor to Google, laid the groundwork for what would become one of the most transformative companies in history.

The chapter delves into the challenges they faced, the late-night coding sessions, and the moment when the concept of PageRank was conceived—a breakthrough that would revolutionize internet search and set the stage for the rise of Google.

From Garage to Global Dominance

As Google emerged from the confines of a Silicon Valley garage, the narrative unfolds the challenges and triumphs that accompanied its ascent. Larry Page's visionary leadership style and unyielding commitment to innovation are explored in detail, painting a vivid picture of the company's evolution from a scrappy startup to a global powerhouse.

The chapter touches on Google's IPO, the development of iconic products like Gmail and Google Maps, and the company's unrelenting pursuit of organizing the world's information.

The Mind Unraveled

The central theme of the chapter revolves around Larry Page's unique approach to problem-solving and his relentless pursuit of ambitious goals.

Through interviews with colleagues, friends, and industry experts, the narrative peels back the layers of Page's mind, exploring the blend of audacity and pragmatism that fueled his success.

The chapter concludes with a teaser, setting the stage for the subsequent exploration of Larry Page's impact on the technology landscape and the intriguing challenges that lay ahead in unraveling the mind of this enigmatic visionary.

2

The Architect of Tomorrow

The Moonshot Factory

The chapter opens with a glimpse into X, Google's moonshot factory, where Larry Page's penchant for tackling audacious challenges reaches its zenith. From self-driving cars to smart contact lenses, the narrative unfolds the diverse projects incubated within X, providing readers with a front-row seat to the intersection of technology and imagination.

Delving into Larry Page's role in fostering a culture of innovation, the chapter explores the principles that guide X's moonshot projects and the impact they have on shaping the future.

The Alphabet Gambit

As Google evolves, Larry Page orchestrates a strategic reorganization, creating Alphabet Inc. The chapter navigates the complexities of this corporate restructuring, examining the motivations behind it and the ripple effects it sends through the tech industry. Through interviews with key players in the restructuring process, readers gain insight into Page's vision for a more streamlined and diversified conglomerate.

A Visionary's Dilemma

The narrative explores the dichotomy of Larry Page's role as both a visionary and a leader grappling with the challenges of managing a colossal corporation. It delves into the tensions between innovation and stability, autonomy and cohesion, shedding light on the delicate balance Page strives to maintain.

Through anecdotes and behind-the-scenes accounts, the chapter captures moments of internal strife, decision-making dilemmas, and the high stakes of navigating Google's transformation into Alphabet.

Beyond the Silicon Valley Bubble

The chapter broadens its scope to Larry Page's global impact and his vision for technology's role in addressing pressing global issues. It examines initiatives like Google.org, exploring Page's commitment to using technology as a force for good.

The narrative delves into Page's advocacy for renewable energy, healthcare innovation, and his belief in the transformative power of technology to address societal challenges. Through interviews with philanthropic partners and industry experts, readers gain insights into the broader implications of Page's vision beyond the tech landscape.

The Personal Side of Larry Page

Closing the chapter, the narrative takes a more intimate turn, offering a glimpse into the personal life of Larry Page. From his family dynamics to his hobbies and interests outside the tech sphere, the chapter humanizes the visionary figure, presenting a more rounded portrait of the man behind the technology empire.

The chapter concludes by leaving readers with a sense of anticipation, setting the stage for the exploration of Larry Page's legacy and the challenges that lie ahead in the next chapter, promising a deeper understanding of the mind that continues to shape the future.

3

Legacy and Lessons

Shaping the Digital Landscape

The chapter opens with an exploration of Larry Page's enduring impact on the digital landscape. It traces the evolution of Google and Alphabet under his leadership, highlighting key milestones, acquisitions, and strategic decisions that shaped the tech giant into the influential force it is today.

The narrative delves into Google's expansion into artificial intelligence, machine learning, and cloud computing, showcasing how Larry Page's vision propelled the company to the forefront of technological innovation.

The Dark Side of the Moonshot

While Larry Page's moonshot projects have garnered praise, the chapter also confronts the challenges and controversies that accompanied some of these ambitious ventures. From ethical concerns surrounding Google's data practices to the regulatory scrutiny faced by Alphabet, the narrative navigates the complexities of maintaining innovation while addressing societal and ethical considerations.

Through interviews with industry experts, policymakers, and Alphabet insiders, readers gain a nuanced understanding of the ethical dilemmas that arise when pushing the boundaries of technology.

Lessons in Leadership

The chapter shifts focus to Larry Page's leadership style, analyzing the strengths and weaknesses that defined his tenure at Google and Alphabet. Drawing on interviews with colleagues and industry analysts, the narrative dissects Page's approach to decision-making, risk-taking, and fostering a culture of innovation.

The exploration of leadership challenges, such as internal tensions and external criticisms, provides valuable insights for aspiring leaders and entrepreneurs navigating the ever-evolving landscape of the tech industry.

The Unfinished Symphony

As Larry Page steps back from day-to-day responsibilities at Alphabet, the narrative reflects on the legacy he leaves behind and the challenges that remain. The chapter explores the ongoing impact of Page's vision on Alphabet's trajectory, examining how his influence continues to shape the company's culture and strategic direction.

Through interviews with current leaders at Alphabet and industry observers, readers gain a sense of the ongoing narrative of Google and Alphabet beyond Larry Page's direct involvement.

Looking Forward

Closing the chapter, the narrative contemplates the future of technology and innovation, considering the lessons learned from Larry Page's journey. The chapter challenges readers to ponder the role of visionary leaders in shaping the trajectory of industries and society at large, setting the stage for a broader exploration of the intersection between technology and humanity in the concluding chapters.

The chapter concludes with a sense of reflection, leaving readers with a deeper understanding of Larry Page's legacy and the enduring impact of his contributions to the ever-evolving world of technology.

4

Beyond the Search Box: Technology, Humanity, and the Future

The Human Side of Innovation

The chapter opens with a broader exploration of the relationship between technology and humanity, examining the societal implications of the innovations pioneered by Larry Page and his contemporaries. It delves into the evolving role of technology in our daily lives, addressing both the positive and negative aspects of the digital revolution.

Through interviews with thought leaders, ethicists, and technology experts, the narrative paints a nuanced picture of the complex interplay between human values and technological progress.

Navigating Ethical Frontiers

Building on the ethical considerations introduced in previous chapters, this section of the narrative delves deeper into the ethical frontiers of technology. It explores how Larry Page's legacy at Google and Alphabet contributed to the ongoing conversation about privacy, data security, and the responsible development of emerging technologies like artificial intelligence.

The chapter invites readers to ponder the ethical dilemmas that arise as technology becomes increasingly intertwined with the fabric of society, challenging them to consider the responsibilities of both individual users and tech corporations.

The Evolving Ecosystem

As the tech landscape continues to evolve, the chapter examines the emergence of new players, disruptive technologies, and shifting paradigms. It explores the impact of advancements in areas such as quantum computing, biotechnology, and the Internet of Things on the future of innovation.

Through interviews with industry insiders and trend analysts, the narrative provides a glimpse into the ever-changing landscape of technology and its potential to reshape industries and societies.

Lessons for the Next Generation

The chapter shifts focus to the next generation of entrepreneurs and innovators, distilling key lessons from Larry Page's journey. It explores the qualities that define successful leaders in the dynamic world of technology and offers insights for aspiring visionaries seeking to make a positive impact on the world.

Through anecdotes, case studies, and interviews with emerging leaders, the narrative provides a roadmap for navigating the challenges and opportunities that lie ahead in the ever-accelerating pace of technological advancement.

The Enduring Legacy

Closing the chapter, the narrative reflects on the enduring legacy of Larry Page and the contributions of visionaries who have shaped the technological landscape. It challenges readers to consider their role in influencing the trajectory of innovation and fostering a harmonious relationship between technology and humanity.

The chapter concludes with a call to action, encouraging readers to actively participate in the ongoing dialogue about the future of technology and its impact on society, ensuring that the legacy of visionaries like Larry Page continues to inspire positive change in the world.

5

Future Horizons: Navigating the Unknown

The Next Wave of Innovation

The chapter opens with a panoramic view of the technological horizon, exploring the frontiers of innovation that lie beyond the present. It delves into emerging technologies, such as augmented reality, decentralized computing, and breakthroughs in renewable energy, offering readers a glimpse into the next wave of transformative advancements.

Through conversations with industry pioneers and futurists, the narrative paints a picture of a future where technology is seamlessly integrated into every aspect of our lives.

The Intersection of Technology and Humanity

Building on the themes introduced in earlier chapters, this section of the narrative examines the evolving relationship between technology and humanity. It explores how innovations in fields like healthcare, education, and communication have the potential to enhance the human experience while also addressing the ethical considerations and societal impacts that accompany these advancements.

Through case studies and expert interviews, the chapter fosters a deeper understanding of how technology can be harnessed for the betterment of society.

The Global Technological Landscape

The narrative broadens its scope to the global stage, exploring how technology is shaping economies, cultures, and geopolitical dynamics. It examines the role of multinational tech corporations, the rise of innovation hubs in unexpected places, and the challenges and opportunities presented by a globally connected world.

Through interviews with international leaders and experts, readers gain insights into the diverse ways in which technology is influencing societies around the globe.

The Quest for Sustainability

Addressing one of the defining challenges of the 21st century, the chapter explores the intersection of technology and sustainability. It examines how innovative solutions, from clean energy initiatives to sustainable agriculture practices, are driving efforts to mitigate the impact of climate change and create a more sustainable future.

Through interviews with environmental advocates, scientists, and technology leaders, the narrative sheds light on the pivotal role technology plays in addressing the pressing challenges of our time.

Charting a Course for Tomorrow

Closing the chapter, the narrative shifts focus to the collective responsibility of individuals, corporations, and governments in shaping the future. It encourages readers to actively engage in conversations about the ethical, social, and environmental implications of technology, emphasizing the importance of fostering a collaborative and inclusive approach to innovation.

The chapter concludes with a call to envision a future where technology is harnessed for the collective good, challenging readers to be active participants in shaping a world where the potential of technology is realized for the benefit of all.

6

Reimagining Tomorrow: The Intersection of Technology, Ethics, and Humanity

The Ethical Imperative

The chapter opens with a profound exploration of the ethical considerations that permeate the rapidly advancing world of technology. It delves into the responsibilities of innovators, corporations, and policymakers in navigating the ethical landscape, addressing issues such as algorithmic bias, data privacy, and the societal impact of emerging technologies.

Through interviews with ethicists, tech leaders, and policymakers, the narrative invites readers to reflect on the ethical imperatives that should guide the development and deployment of technology in an increasingly interconnected world.

The Human-Centered Revolution

Building on the ethical discourse, this section of the narrative emphasizes the importance of a human-centered approach to technology. It explores how design thinking, empathy, and inclusivity can shape the development of technologies that enhance the human experience and contribute to the well-being of diverse communities.

Case studies and interviews with designers, psychologists, and social scientists provide insights into how a focus on human values can lead to more ethical and sustainable technological solutions.

The Collaborative Future

The chapter shifts its focus to the collaborative nature of innovation, exploring how interdisciplinary partnerships and global cooperation are essential in addressing complex challenges. It highlights the role of open-source initiatives, public-private collaborations, and international efforts in fostering innovation that transcends borders.

Through stories of successful collaborations and insights from global leaders, the narrative emphasizes the need for a united approach to solving the intricate problems that lie ahead.

Education and Empowerment

As technology continues to evolve, the narrative explores the vital role of education in empowering individuals to navigate the digital landscape. It examines innovative approaches to education, the democratization of knowledge through online platforms, and the importance of fostering digital literacy.

Through interviews with educators, ed-tech pioneers, and thought leaders, the chapter inspires readers to envision a future where education becomes a catalyst for positive change in society.

The Call for Responsible Innovation

Closing the chapter, the narrative synthesizes the key themes of ethics, humanity, collaboration, and education into a call for responsible innovation. It challenges readers to actively contribute to shaping a future where technology aligns with human values, enhances global well-being, and fosters a sustainable and inclusive world.

The chapter concludes with a sense of optimism, inviting readers to embrace their roles as stewards of the future, actively engaging in the ongoing dialogue about the intersection of technology, ethics, and humanity.

7

The Uncharted Frontier: Exploring the Unknown

Quantum Leaps in Computing

The chapter opens with a dive into the uncharted territory of quantum computing. It explores the potential of quantum technologies to revolutionize computation, solve problems deemed unsolvable by classical computers, and usher in a new era of scientific discovery and innovation.

Through conversations with quantum physicists, researchers, and industry leaders, the narrative provides insights into the current state of quantum computing and the profound implications it holds for the future of technology.

The Promise of Biotechnology

Building on the exploration of quantum computing, this section of the narrative delves into the frontier of biotechnology. It examines breakthroughs in genetic engineering, personalized medicine, and the convergence of biology and computing, offering readers a glimpse into a future where advancements in biotechnology reshape healthcare, agriculture, and our understanding of life itself.

Through interviews with biotechnologists, medical researchers, and ethicists, the chapter explores the promises and ethical considerations inherent in the ongoing biotechnological revolution.

Space: The Next Innovation Frontier

The narrative expands its scope to the cosmos, exploring the burgeoning space industry and the transformative impact of space exploration on technology and humanity. It delves into private space companies, the race to colonize Mars, and the potential for space-based technologies to address challenges on Earth.

Through conversations with space entrepreneurs, astronomers, and visionaries, readers gain insights into the exciting possibilities and ethical considerations associated with the space frontier.

The Convergence of Realities

As technology continues to advance, the chapter explores the convergence of physical and virtual realities. It examines the evolution of augmented and virtual reality technologies, their applications in various industries, and the potential for immersive experiences to reshape how we interact with the world.

Through interviews with VR/AR developers, futurists, and experts in human-computer interaction, the narrative paints a vivid picture of a future where the boundaries between the physical and virtual worlds blur.

Reflections on the Uncharted

Closing the chapter, the narrative reflects on the common threads that weave through these uncharted frontiers. It emphasizes the importance of ethical considerations, global collaboration, and a human-centered approach in navigating the unknown.

The chapter concludes by inviting readers to contemplate their roles in shaping the future, encouraging them to engage in the ongoing dialogue about the uncharted territories of technology and their impact on the trajectory of humanity.

8

The Tapestry of Tomorrow: Weaving a Shared Future

Uniting the Global Narrative

The chapter opens with an exploration of the interconnected nature of the global technological narrative. It examines how innovations in one corner of the world reverberate across borders, shaping the collective future. Through stories of collaboration, knowledge exchange, and shared challenges, the narrative illustrates the importance of a united global perspective in navigating the complexities of tomorrow.

The Imperative of Inclusivity

Building on the theme of global unity, this section of the narrative emphasizes the imperative of inclusivity in the development and deployment of technology. It explores how diverse voices, perspectives, and experiences contribute to more equitable and sustainable innovations.

Through interviews with advocates for diversity and inclusion, the chapter delves into initiatives and strategies that aim to ensure that the benefits of technology are accessible to all, regardless of background or geography.

A Sustainable Tomorrow

The narrative shifts its focus to the crucial role of sustainability in shaping the future. It explores how technological advancements can be harnessed to address environmental challenges, promote sustainable practices, and create a harmonious balance between human activities and the planet.

Through conversations with environmentalists, sustainability experts, and innovators, the chapter presents stories of initiatives that leverage technology for the betterment of both humanity and the Earth.

Digital Empowerment and Global Citizenship

As technology becomes increasingly integral to our lives, the chapter explores the concept of digital empowerment and its role in fostering global citizenship. It delves into the ways technology can empower individuals to contribute positively to society, bridge cultural divides, and participate in the shared responsibility of shaping a better future.

Through interviews with digital activists, social entrepreneurs, and educators, the narrative inspires readers to harness the potential of technology as a tool for positive global impact.

The Ethical Tech Covenant

Closing the chapter, the narrative proposes the concept of an Ethical Tech Covenant—a shared commitment among individuals, corporations, and governments to prioritize ethical considerations in the development and deployment of technology. It explores how such a covenant could serve as a guiding framework for navigating the complexities of the technological landscape.

The chapter concludes with a call to action, encouraging readers to embrace their roles as architects of the future, actively contributing to the weaving of a tapestry where technology, ethics, and humanity converge for the benefit of all.

9

Resilience in the Face of Disruption

The Dynamics of Disruption

The chapter opens with an exploration of the inevitability of disruption in the fast-paced world of technology. It examines historical examples of industry-shifting disruptions and the characteristics that define resilient individuals, organizations, and societies in the face of rapid change.

Through case studies and interviews with leaders who have weathered disruptive forces, the narrative provides insights into the principles of resilience and adaptability.

Innovating Through Adversity

Building on the theme of resilience, this section of the narrative delves into the concept of innovation amid adversity. It explores how challenges, crises, and disruptions can serve as catalysts for creative problem-solving and the emergence of groundbreaking solutions.

Through stories of companies that have thrived in the midst of adversity and interviews with innovation experts, the chapter encourages readers to view disruptions as opportunities for positive transformation.

The Human Element in Tech Resilience

The narrative shifts its focus to the human element of resilience in the technology landscape. It explores the psychological factors that contribute to individual and collective resilience, emphasizing the importance of emotional intelligence, collaboration, and a growth mindset in navigating turbulent times.

Through interviews with psychologists, leadership coaches, and tech professionals who have overcome personal and professional challenges, the chapter provides a deeper understanding of the human dimensions of resilience.

The Role of Technology in Crisis Response

As the world grapples with various crises, the chapter examines the role of technology in crisis response and recovery. It explores how innovations in areas such as communication, healthcare, and disaster management have played crucial roles in mitigating the impact of crises and fostering resilience.

Through case studies and interviews with experts in crisis response, the narrative showcases the transformative potential of technology in building resilient communities.

Navigating the Unpredictable

Closing the chapter, the narrative reflects on the uncertainties that lie ahead and the strategies for navigating the unpredictable nature of the technological landscape. It explores the role of strategic planning, agility, and a forward-thinking mindset in building resilience for the future.

The chapter concludes with a call to embrace disruption as an inherent part of the technological journey, encouraging readers to cultivate resilience and adaptability as essential qualities for navigating the ever-changing currents of the tech-driven world.

10

The Human-Tech Symphony: Crafting a Harmonious Future

The Symphony of Interconnected Systems

The chapter opens with a metaphorical exploration of the intricate interplay between technology and humanity, likening it to a symphony of interconnected systems. It delves into how the harmonious integration of these systems can lead to a future where technology enhances human well-being, fosters inclusivity, and promotes sustainable progress.

Through visual metaphors and interviews with experts in various fields, the narrative sets the stage for a vision of a collaborative and balanced relationship between technology and humanity.

From Artificial to Augmented Intelligence

Building on the symphonic metaphor, this section of the narrative examines the evolution of artificial intelligence into augmented intelligence. It explores how AI technologies, when designed with a human-centric approach, can augment human capabilities, foster creativity, and contribute to the betterment of society.

Through discussions with AI researchers, ethicists, and innovators, the chapter paints a picture of a future where intelligent technologies work in harmony with human values.

The Cultural Rhythm of Innovation

The narrative expands its focus to the cultural dimensions of innovation, exploring how diverse cultural perspectives contribute to a rich tapestry of technological advancements. It examines the importance of cultural inclusivity in the development of technology and how embracing a variety of viewpoints can lead to more robust and globally relevant innovations.

Through interviews with cultural experts, anthropologists, and technology leaders, the chapter celebrates the cultural diversity that enriches the human-tech symphony.

Empathy in Design: Crafting User-Centric Solutions

As technology becomes more integrated into our daily lives, the chapter explores the critical role of empathy in design. It examines how user-centric approaches, informed by empathy, can lead to the creation of technologies that resonate with the needs and aspirations of individuals.

Through case studies and conversations with design thinkers, the narrative illustrates how empathy-driven design can humanize technology and contribute to a more user-friendly and accessible digital landscape.

Orchestrating a Sustainable Future

Closing the chapter, the narrative reflects on the imperative of orchestrating a sustainable future. It explores how a harmonious relationship between technology and humanity must prioritize sustainability, environmental responsibility, and the well-being of future generations.

Through discussions with sustainability advocates, environmental scientists, and technology leaders, the chapter emphasizes the need for a collective commitment to building a sustainable and resilient future.

The chapter concludes with a vision of the harmonious symphony that emerges when technology and humanity collaborate seamlessly, inspiring readers to actively contribute to the creation of a future where the human-tech partnership is characterized by balance, inclusivity, and a shared commitment to the greater good.

11

The Compass of Digital Ethics: Navigating the Moral Landscape

The Ethical Compass in a Digital Age

The chapter opens with an exploration of the evolving moral landscape in the digital age. It examines the ethical challenges and considerations that arise as technology becomes increasingly integrated into every facet of human existence. Through real-world examples and thought-provoking scenarios, the narrative sets the stage for a deeper exploration of the ethical dimensions of the digital era.

The Pillars of Digital Ethics

Building on the foundational exploration, this section of the narrative delves into the key pillars that underpin digital ethics. It explores concepts such as privacy, transparency, accountability, and fairness, examining how these principles form the ethical framework guiding responsible technological development and deployment.

Through interviews with ethicists, legal scholars, and technology leaders, the chapter provides insights into the ethical considerations that should shape the decisions of individuals, corporations, and policymakers.

Navigating the Data Dilemma

The narrative shifts its focus to the complex terrain of data ethics. It examines the ethical implications of data collection, storage, and usage, addressing issues such as consent, data ownership, and the potential for misuse. Real-world case studies and expert perspectives shed light on the challenges and opportunities inherent in navigating the data dilemma ethically.

The Human-Centric Imperative

As technology continues to advance, the chapter emphasizes the human-centric imperative within digital ethics. It explores how prioritizing human well-being, inclusivity, and the protection of fundamental rights becomes paramount in designing and deploying technologies responsibly.

Through discussions with user experience experts, human rights advocates, and technology ethicists, the narrative illustrates the importance of placing the human experience at the center of ethical considerations.

Governance in the Digital Realm

Closing the chapter, the narrative reflects on the role of governance in ensuring ethical practices within the digital realm. It explores the need for regulatory frameworks, industry standards, and international collaboration to establish ethical norms that guide the responsible development and use of technology.

Through interviews with policymakers, legal experts, and technology leaders, the chapter encourages readers to engage in the ongoing dialogue about the ethical governance of the digital landscape.

The chapter concludes with a call to action, inspiring individuals, corporations, and policymakers to uphold the principles of digital ethics as a compass guiding the responsible and ethical integration of technology into our lives.

12

The Technological Renaissance: Crafting a Humanistic Future

The Renaissance of Human-Centric Technology

The chapter opens with a vision of a technological renaissance—a period where innovation is driven by a deep commitment to human values and the betterment of society. It explores how a renaissance mindset can inspire the creation of technologies that not only advance human progress but also contribute to the collective flourishing of humanity.

Through narratives of transformative technologies and interviews with thought leaders, the chapter sets the stage for a humanistic renaissance in the world of technology.

Cultivating Digital Empathy

Building on the theme of humanism, this section of the narrative delves into the concept of digital empathy. It explores how fostering empathy in the digital realm can lead to technologies that are more attuned to human emotions, needs, and diverse perspectives.

Through case studies and discussions with empathy advocates, the chapter illustrates the transformative potential of infusing technology with a sense of understanding and compassion.

The Inclusive Innovation Ecosystem

The narrative broadens its scope to explore the concept of an inclusive innovation ecosystem. It examines how creating environments that celebrate diversity, foster collaboration, and prioritize accessibility can lead to a more inclusive and equitable technological landscape.

Through interviews with leaders in inclusive innovation and diversity advocates, the chapter showcases initiatives and strategies that contribute to building a technology ecosystem that benefits everyone.

Technology and the Arts: A Creative Fusion

As technology and the arts converge, the chapter explores the creative fusion that results from this intersection. It examines how the collaboration between technologists and artists can lead to the development of innovative, aesthetically pleasing, and culturally resonant technologies.

Through discussions with tech-art innovators, the narrative provides insights into the symbiotic relationship between technology and the arts in shaping a richer and more expressive future.

Crafting a Legacy of Ethical Innovation

Closing the chapter, the narrative reflects on the legacy of ethical innovation and the impact it can have on shaping the future. It explores how individuals, corporations, and policymakers can contribute to a positive legacy by prioritizing ethical considerations, sustainability, and the well-being of both humanity and the planet.

The chapter concludes with a vision of a future where the technological renaissance thrives, guided by humanistic principles, ethical innovation, and a shared commitment to creating a world where technology and humanity coexist harmoniously for the benefit of all.

13

Summary

In this book, we embark on a comprehensive journey through the life and mind of Larry Page, co-founder of Google and influential figure in the tech industry. The chapters unfold Larry Page's early life, his partnership with Sergey Brin at Stanford, the evolution of Google, and the transformation of Alphabet. We explore his visionary leadership, moonshot projects, and the broader impact of Google's innovations on the global technological landscape.

As we progress, the narrative expands to encompass the broader themes of technology and humanity, addressing ethical considerations, the global impact of innovation, and the responsibilities of leaders in the tech realm. The chapters delve into emerging technologies like quantum computing, biotechnology, and space exploration, presenting a vivid picture of the uncharted frontiers that lie ahead.

The book emphasizes the need for ethical frameworks in the digital age, exploring the pillars of digital ethics such as privacy, transparency, and accountability. It navigates the complexities of data ethics, human-centric design, and the role of governance in ensuring responsible technology development.

Towards the end, the narrative paints a vision of a technological renaissance—

a future where innovation is driven by humanistic principles, empathy, and inclusivity. It explores the creative fusion of technology and the arts, the importance of diversity in innovation ecosystems, and the legacy of ethical innovation that can shape a positive future.

Ultimately, the book invites readers to actively participate in shaping the harmonious relationship between technology and humanity, urging them to navigate the challenges of the digital age with a compass of ethical considerations, empathy, and a shared commitment to a better future.

www.ingramcontent.com/pod-product-compliance
Lightning Source LLC
LaVergne TN
LVHW020455080526
838202LV00057B/5971